D0873568

YES THORN

Ruth J. Rapp
Minnesota
Writers
Collection

The Tupelo Press First / Second Book Award:
The Berkshire Prize

Jennifer Michael Hecht, *The Last Ancient World*
    Selected by Janet Holmes

Aimee Nezhukumatathil, *Miracle Fruit*
    Selected by Gregory Orr

Bill Van Every, *Devoted Creatures*
    Selected by Thomas Lux

David Petruzelli, *Everyone Coming Toward You*
    Selected by Campbell McGrath

Lillias Bever, *Bellini in Istanbul*
    Selected by Michael Collier

Dwaine Rieves, *When the Eye Forms*
    Selected by Carolyn Forché

Kristin Bock, *Cloisters*
    Selected by David St. John

Jennifer Militello, *Flinch of Song*
    Selected by Carol Ann Davis and Jeffrey Levine

Megan Snyder-Camp, *The Forest of Sure Things*
    Selected by Carol Ann Davis and Jeffrey Levine

Daniel Khalastchi, *Manoleria*
    Selected by Carol Ann Davis and Jeffrey Levine

Mary Molinary, *Mary & the Giant Mechanism*
    Selected by Carol Ann Davis and Jeffrey Levine

Ye Chun, *Lantern Puzzle*
    Selected by D. A. Powell

Kristina Jipson, *Halve*
    Selected by Dan Beachy-Quick

Amy Munson, *Yes Thorn*
    Selected by Paisley Rekdal

YES THORN
AMY MUNSON

TUPELO PRESS | NORTH ADAMS, MASSACHUSETTS

CANCEL

Yes Thorn.
Copyright © 2016 Amy Munson. All rights reserved.

Library of Congress Cataloging-in-Publication Data

Names: Munson, Amy, 1978- author.
Title: Yes thorn / Amy Munson.
Description: North Adams, Massachusetts : Tupelo Press, [2016] | Includes
  bibliographical references.
Identifiers: LCCN 2016039553 | ISBN 9781936797882 (pbk. : alk. paper)
Classification: LCC PS3613.U6928 A6 2016 | DDC 811/.6--dc23

Cover designed by Michael Cina.
Text designed and composed in Granjon by Dede Cummings.

First paperback edition: October 2016.

Epigraph: excerpt of Lorine Niedecker's "Next year or I fly my rounds,
tempestuous" is from *Lorine Niedecker: Collected Works*, edited by Jenny
Penberthy, copyright © 2003 by the Regents of the University of California.
Published by the University of California Press and used with permission.

Other than brief excerpts for reviews and commentaries, no part of this book
may be reproduced by any means without permission of the publisher. Please
address requests for reprint permission or for course-adoption discounts to:

TUPELO PRESS
P.O. Box 1767, North Adams, Massachusetts 01247
Telephone: (413) 664-9611 / editor@tupelopress.org / www.tupelopress.org

Tupelo Press is an award-winning independent literary press that publishes
fine fiction, nonfiction, and poetry in books that are a joy to hold as well as
read. Tupelo Press is a registered 501(c)(3) nonprofit organization, and we
rely on public support to carry out our mission of publishing extraordinary
work that may be outside the realm of the large commercial publishers.
Financial donations are welcome and are tax deductible.

Amy (McCann) Munson is a fiscal year 2014 recipient of an
Artist Initiative grant from the Minnesota State Arts Board.
This activity is made possible by the voters of Minnesota through
a grant from the Minnesota State Arts Board, thanks to a
legislative appropriation by the Minnesota State Legislature's
clean water, land, and legacy amendment and by a grant from
the National Endowment for the Arts.

ART WORKS.
arts.gov

Jesus, I'm
going out
and throw
my arms
around.

— Lorine Niedecker

Contents

I

ALTRICIAL

What offers
a skeletal peep.
Feather smear,
mostly gullet—
agape for the secondhand
upchuck grub,
bolus crammed iridescent
with carapace and wing.
A holiness, this
helplessness,
the mother's tireless,
kenotic reconnaissance
ending every time
with her head bent to
her nest of tidbit beggars,
X-ray translucent,
the tinder of their bones
radiant beneath.
All hollow. The aerate
marrow, the grand
opening of brand-new
guts, the gimme
litany squalling from
the eternal central yawn,
the same way I wake
each morning crumpled and
ravenous, limbs stilted
as puppetry, to light
like an afterbirth,
wondering if the soul's
a vestigial investment.
If the sky—bloodshot,
placental—is beginning
or ending. What might fall,
when I wail, from above
toward my wide-open mouth.

RIFT

The skull's cunning
way of slowly closing
to fortress its softest

parts. All that feels
fontanel—our fathers
forgetting birthdays,

those middle-school
girls who saw me only
through a petechial haze,

ready to rip my hair
at the root. Once earth
did this in reverse:

one congealed continent
levered separate, the world
now seven times more

vulnerable, very little able
to hurdle the blue
between each ragged

island. Inside, alive,
our bones aren't dry,
but hived—a fizz of cells.

Blood sponge. Openings
to make us more
accommodating. Every

day when I didn't know
what would or wouldn't
come for me, I waited

at the entrance, parka
zipped to the throat.
Behind me, the custodian

shuffled loose-leaf,
lunch sacks, F tests
into his bin. Forehead

to safety glass, I strained
for a familiar car, latitudes
and longitudes of mesh

graphing the view, suggesting
a geometry contrary to those
irregular, unguarded places

we're born into—the uncertain
father, the girls who lock
their hands in fists

all day under desks,
even though their hate stays
indefinite. Even though their nails
break their own skin.

Congenital

Inside every heart
slumps the same
silk-fleshed fig

bitten in the first
lost garden. First
relinquishing skin.

Our paradox: carrion
that carries on,
tomb that mushrooms

to coax its stone
aside, and inside
gauze, deflated,

suggests the grave
we deserve yet
can never reenter.

Our central distortion.
Our sweet-weakened
teeth, long toiling

in fields, our orphaned
forever—tended then
bereft of fruit. A blush

inflames the slack-winged
birds, our half-mast
tails slapping the base

of our spines in migrant
flight. Our compass
slagging south. Sour

glint of bile. The pinch
of gilt—belated reflex—
diapered by our appetites.

Where Were You First Introduced to the Spirit?

Like a white gauze
dress I couldn't lift off—

maybe it locked on
while he held me under,

its hundred buttons
minnowing shut.

Clouds like coffin lilies.
Light stuttered, a struck dove.

I emerged blank and
intimate, invisibly bridal

beneath a twang of blue,
knowing how it felt

to be surrounded—water
forever a conveyor

of start over, a curtain
that cannot be torn,

that can be torn, over and over—

CORSETRY

Everything pinned to this bodice
a brooch *in memoriam* of—

at the left shoulder a hazard

                         of crows; skein of geese at the right.

Bittersweet branch

              at the base of my throat.

Pollen dusts
the hoisted breasts; between,
a cluster of thumbnail plums
in their tarnished, glaucous skins.   And my skin

pintucked   by crossed grosgrain:
                      pucker and swell,

then an iliac knot.   Stubbed lungs.   My ligature—

someone's unseen signature
basted in

        along the boning.

These inclusions:
        Feathers from a ruptured eider.
        Cirrus edge of lace to garnish seams.

And a milliner's rose, starched-blue
organza, and in the inner pocket a photograph of
breath in winter,   the interrupting
                       static of snow . . .

A ring constricts a finger, and ribbon
        diminishes the wrist;

the organs are parsed
in the divided
        drawers of ribs—

This shadowbox. This piecework. This way

               my waist contracts

without hands to span it.

Amor

Was it the street market in Monterrey—
the bonito's eye, unlashed, a tarnished,
mercurial hatch? The ice beneath
the piled fish pinked. When you asked me
to pick which we'd eat, I shunned them.
Minus their chummed guts, each was
slender and clean. In that rank heat.
That lurid, commercial snarl. I downed
broth spiked with cacti, sucked honeycomb
until its amber drape threatened to fossil
my gawking maw. Foolish to think
it matters how I lost you. As if choosing
one carcass over another could alter
a future. I grew up cold-cocking sunnies
I'd palmed from the lake—braining them
against the dock with no intent for food,
just some unnamed grain of harm
within me, integral as salt. What organ
is it that balances a swimming fish? You
waved me over, your hand a vacant
invitation. Inside me, the flail
of discrepancies—how not choosing
becomes choosing not to, how any flex
in a mirror estranges the body. Even
alive, the eye's curve refuses to project
a wanted world above the real. I saw
nothing in the eye of that fish—no
face, no flash of diving light, no
net impending, no drag of rope
winched to the soaked deck. I saw no
entrance, but a breach—the way
breaking down a door means
you'll never truly get inside
It was April. A Saturday. We were
hungry, far-flung, and strangely
alone, nowhere near the ocean.

SALT WIFE

Cured to permanent gown, a mineral
seep—all tears, all weep. The lick I am.

The lips I'll crimp in the swap
of elements—the more of them,

the more I melt. My backdrop
old smoke in the shape of tents,

my city most flagrant in absence—
gutted cavity under the SOS of stars.

I have been sustained by distant fires.
I have harbored desire for deciduous places.

I put everything I loved behind me.
If you kiss me, the taste of drowning.

Winter Cutting

How to reckon propagation when
sun leaks a measly dose,
when the blanched tangle

of new roots goes
ingrown in its bottle on the sill.
Nearby, a wooden bowl holds

a pliable number of plums. Always in
the flesh the thorn. The fruit
pustuled around its invasion.

Find in the crow's rickety throat
a shard of seed—unutterable
hull. Sprout a plum pit

and that tree's the offspring
of just half its graft—sour enough
to sprain the tongue.

Some days the body made
between us—its welds,
its doubled joints—slows us,

though both hearts rabbit in
our pressed-against chests. Blood's
arboreal throb. Nothing comes

from nothing; every color's hidden
in a single black feather,
in what light does to snow,

facets rendered visible
by collision. The garden
I wanted suspended in glass

for as long as planting promises loss.

CHAMBERING

We go toward gardens. Regardless
of distance, we can rest

the moon on our palms, closing
one eye to see more clearly.

We've been alive much longer
than flowers. Hope seeps between

our fingers—frigid, borrowed light.

—

How occult it feels to be
near you in dark places:

your basement during a blackout,
your garden once the lantern's

wicked through its pool of oil,
when you thumb its residue,

slick crescent on my cheek.

—

Interference leaves me fierce.
Curse your straying kiss,

your elsewhere. How finely
honed this loneliness. Out back,

bindweed finds the clothesline,
wrenching itself ever more

tightly around the rope.

—

Sanguine, plants harbor
water as blood. Steep

sustenance from mud.
If an element of uncertainty

tenses a tame scene to art,
what elevation arises from

all we lodge in rot?

—

Prize out the fruit, and the plant
might quit—a vacant chamber

can't keep sweet. We tongued
seeds from sockets, burying

any hope of new cherries.
We burrowed our names

deep into trees, desiring history.

—

We chase fertility in
chemistry. Together, our skin

wicks—salt to preserve, heat
to rivet. Even with the risk

of your silence, even in the curse
of my grasping, I'm most lovely

inside your body.

—

Though we value nothing
over flowers, we tend to weeds

most closely—careful not
to spare a shred of root

as we evict their squat,
enduring hearts, squander

those who would overtake us.

XX

Lust's albumen. The summer inside
girls' thighs.
           The wraparound

porch overcome with ivy,
the earliest a.m. stop-motion

blossom and collapse of
bindweed in every ditch and
abandoned bed.
           Below in the dirt

hide buttons lost by ghosts, ivory
buttons that, thumbed shut,
trapped damp waists again in skirts.

The lure of what's kept under.
The pressing against, the public feel
of summer.
           July swells the frame

until the side door won't bolt tight.
The white-noise whine of cicada
and engine, burr of pollen in

the lung. The lounging, decelerate
heart, ready for any strange entrance.

Oology

How many number a clutch.
What collection of calcium

christening gowns, klatsched
in the cleft of a nest in

a world where, even securely
strapped by chalazae, it seems

safest to be sat on: mice climb vines,
squirrels high-wire limb to limb,

the broom-wielding homeowner
too sick of being dive-bombed

not to swat that rude cradle—dead

brood, Pollocked on the sidewalk,
a series of gooey, irregular moons.

CUR

It was barbeque and grape soda
in the graveyard, a Louisiana
truck-stop tiger, two-for-ones

at a strapless Tallahassee
ladies' night, then crashing
in someone's vinyl recliner

while his dingy Bichon wrestled
leftover ribs from a Styrofoam clamshell.
The next morning, everything

kudzu-blunted. Every other town,
a plywood sign for the evening
hymn sing. I wanted to retch

my drive-thru biscuit breakfast.
I'd passed, in the local parlance,
too many chances to clamp

my collar on a gator. My lot
now to wander—past
a pestilence of billboards

hawking just-like-home
cooking, flea-market grottos
of salvaged antlers and china angels,

litters of demented kittens—
wishing for a kiss to compass me.
Somewhere a girl didn't know

about her tumor. Her father
mowing the lawn, his last
tedious day. I wanted to be

harrowed, hoisted like an innocent.
To revolve dove-high, above it all,
escaping yet condemned enough

to cure and to carry the punishing crowd.

PRAYER

The evangelical exotic-dance instructor considers it
a tent-making ministry. She's squawking her
sweating inner thighs against a portable pole,
her Lucite platform spikes empty as post-
iconoclastic reliquaries looted of holy
molars. God, she's good, if a little bulbous beneath
the elastic of her 32DDD. I'm staring into her
sequins, certain I'll be the vanishing
point of my family's hereditary chill,
the eventual extinction of our milk-
blooded line. Tell me again about your sister
oil-rushing to some eastern Montana
reservation double-wide, how vital it feels
to be ungoverned. To prophesy early
retirement, forty-five and flush with easy,
greasy cash. This lady on the black-box stage is
so solo in her sex. Her lacquered manicure,
the inverted invitation of her, but no one's close
enough to touch. They toss dollars, taking up
a collection. Our parents couldn't keep it
together—mine, done before I was born,
stayed so I could grow up in a house
of ghosts; yours celebrated their fifty-second
anniversary with a serving of papers.
As if you can escape, once you're soldered—
bolted tight, then a keloid weld. God knows
I've tried to fling my legs around any stable
thing, but it's never my polarity. Remind me
how the whores are always first in line
to commiserate with what's holy.

The Company of Animals

I once bought the bluff
of a man who called me
lovely as a stranger
in a raincoat, the sound
of soda spilling in a movie house.

As the matinee starlet's extravagant,
luminous chin shivered
with devotion, that's how

I watched him, convinced. If the body could disappear—

If a second world—

If the scrim of sense between us, thin
as cigarette paper . . .

But still the impenetrable
caul of sky.
Lingering muck of birth.

In the silent film, white words
scratched and stuttered, uncertain

birds. Also my heart then
was a bird flying

through snowbanks. Also a bird
on an altar in the company of animals

halved for sacrifice: spotless goats
and lambs without blemish, bisected symbols
of a covenant. O what we break, what a hungry

God, what blood we lose
in proving love.

SEE COAST HURRYING INTO SEA

Didn't it doily me? Wave-lace
tatting my ankles in an uneven

hem. A forgotten umbrella, a foraging
for shells—those vacant, softly

howling dwellings. I eaved
my white face with a flyer

from the Hare Krishna parade;
I napped and let grit collect

in any sticky location. It's tough
to graft a turret to a collapsing

tidal castle. Every tourist spoils
a gull. We're flat out here

without our clothes, our jewelry
or eyeglasses, our birthmarks

darkening in the glare. I made
a taxonomy of beach trash: scale,

claw, single unpinned wing.
So many kids pissed in the water

it didn't matter. Fake coconut stink.
I suckled a sweating bottle as a plane

overhead flapped a banner for beer.
I was finally small as a souvenir.

ICARIAN

Gulls puncture the blue between
kites: translucent, cross-boned

animals leashed
to each child's wrist.

Some unusual flyers: octopus,
brontosaur. A man taking Polaroids

alternates between his stumbling
toddler and a sea-star

suckling basalt. The water endless
tics, trinkets of light. I soothe my palm

over sand, try to erase
any evidence of our being

terrestrial. Matted feathers
barb the surface, nib my palm.

O cosseter, O caravel! I am fast-
bound for far shores, already failing

to find the desired—anise,
apricots impossible in this soil.

I'll spend tonight chastely
kissing our limitations, bunked

beside you, a board braced
between us, my affection

folding into itself, into
something unlikely

yet airborne—diamonds of tissue,
tape, and string, delicate

harness for the invisible,
variable currents. Everything given,

one way or another,
a working wing.

The One Sentence You Send Me
from Wisconsin Concerns Chickens

That brood stashed indoors to span
a cold May may never quit worrying
your heels. Once a pet, it's perpetual
nip. My unanswered letters become

their own sad back-talk: Dear,
I'm now convinced it's impossible for us
not to shadow each other, our projected
silhouettes extending into animals

in easy-to-decipher tableaux—
your Great Dane looming over
my calico; my rabbit snared
slack in the jaw of your panther.

I've enclosed a photo of me in
a devastating fur collar, as when
you return I'll be unrecognizably
lavish, unlikely to attend to your lens.

Complain to me then about the chickens,
their bobbling lust for sustenance—
how they ignored fields fattened with worms
to wrestle and prattle for whatever
scraps you'd cooped in your soggy palm.

ACTS OF GOD

In Dakota the wheat's gone
swaybacked with wind. We sleep
on the screened porch to hear the garden

thrash in the air's rough tide, the hiss
of scales as garter snakes twist past
stems, slough their narrow undersides
on stones.

The almanac
pages of our dreams—

Crescent moon: a mouth
open for the sifted grain
of stars.

Quartered-apple moon: a man stoops to plant
lit candles in the hundred jars
he's settled into the field's furrows.

Moon like a doorknob: the sky
swings open, a closet
of identical black suits.

And the rest—knock-kneed moon, birdhouse door, dusty
stopwatch-face, bitter curl of rind, angled moon
of carpentry and reverence, of cobbling together
a ladder or bringing a body
from seed—we find them

behind our eyes
nights. Find when we
cast off the chaff

of sleep: a blue sky,
skidding clouds. Shining

onyx thoraxes of crickets
shaken from the grass.
Splinters of weathered red wood.

Not our fault, we think.

Let the farmers in their diners take
their coffee black and scalding,
scapegoat the weather. Whatever

we've forgotten, for this
we won't be blamed.

FACE OF CLAY

I was never near
pretty. Put me
in girl-bird colors,
base metals to
green my fingers.
Nest me in.
Never in summers
a lifeguard—pale
and dense of thigh,
a weak whistle. I was
the throw-her-in-
the-monkey-pen
playground target,
zoo fare. I kept instead
a bedroom aquarium:
steady temperature,
the delicate algal flush,
found stones and shells
brighter underwater.
My mother'd deliver
sliced cold sandwiches.
I'd flute through my window
an uneven phrase
for the neighbor boy,
imagine his polio-
stolen legs into motion,
his iron lung making
me nervous as a question.
Crickets gnawed nights.
The moon's exoskeletal
glare. Augusts I'd watch
the mechanical parade
of the not-yet-
assembled Jesuit carnival:
trailers of scaffolding,
lights and wires, my hand
making the shape of a
wrench as I thought about

the radial steel spine
of the Ferris wheel,
all weekend in upended
orbit, giving everyone
a flex in the gut, a swinging,
panoramic blink.

3

LOST AUGUST

A gospel boredom. We've sulked
so long this swarthy month, lazy

as chaises, leaking our best salt
until we're dark in every crease,

swiping our eyes with our forearms
for the jolt of the sting. When

the revival takes over our park
with a rented plastic tent,

it gets circus loud—though
instead of an elephant's

penned bellow, the sour
brass smear of a clown's horn,

the whole brouhaha's hoaxing
from the spirit-convex chest of one

snake-legged prophet, yodeling
illegible vowels until his tongue

takes off, swabbing the pollen-
clogged air, agile as an epithet

that shivs its sudden blade
into your softest cleft of flesh.

Under our laughter, our ululating
impressions, some new place

begins to bleed.

POUSTINIA

Say eyes are not the only
eyes. Say others hide

confined behind ribs.
Skull-shod. Say fingerprint

whorls spiral into pupils. Focus
on this. The world

husks itself. Dusts
at a touch.

The scene goes
black as the body

inside skin—the hidden halls,
impossible engines.

You might enter
your desert, the chalky scree

of soul, and stay
until you can stand
it. If you don't

stop crying,
high grass will mask
the sand. But thirst

is no myth: Who will wet
your mouth, if you can find

no eyes, no water?

MARROW

O underneath. O tawdry
sky at dusk, pink and orange fluorescent, loud

rasp of cicadas in the maples—O feeling
in my gut that ousts contentment.

Earlier the air felt gentle, generous
as Saturday. Early in the morning

the air was an institute
of migration: O blackbirds with your lost

feathers pegged in the grass beneath
your roosting trees, branches spackled with seeds and shit,

all day you stream southeast, squabbling
like tourists bound for some boon,

some comedy or glory. O evening sky
flat as violet fondant, I'm terrified

of what I love. What I don't. Of my life
abridged. When I see a thousand dark

bellies of birds, it's like something
to nerve to, a harm that takes me somewhere

free from harm until night comes, chanting
its blood song, pummeled by wings,

trailing me in its curled yellow claws.

God Exists

I take it back.
The dark words my thumb traced

across your skin, that ascending
tenet of faith in ink. The woman

inscribed against you on the bed?
Forget it, you'll never pluck a wife

from some criminal lineup
of bridesmaids. She won't be the one

with a drooling bouquet,
a Midwestern inflection.

I haven't seen an oak tree since
Wisconsin, haven't held

an acorn to your lips and said
remember. *There's no one else*

to join us, you said, *just Hallelujah*
and the laying on of hands. Our

Father. Lay off. I never claimed
I knew the names of children

ringing Sunday bells, never said I'd felt a phantom
pain in my chest where the Spirit once slept.

If I did, if I have, you
were my ghost, my neighbor, my god. I take it

back. I'm no virgin, no star-crossed,
poison-doused lover.

I've left no limestone cairn
at the edge of the frozen river.

Your Heart Your Wobble

Would be in vain. Would be a roadside
soundboard warped with rain, a snare

for whatever's still able to sing—a thousand
scummy sparrows or one feral parakeet

lodged in your hedge, burlesquing
its citrus tail. Would that you were

calla white and hundreds down, invisible,
unable to scrape or escape me. Your pinned

arm, your hand bandage. Our vocabulary
reduced to what can be shouted

up or down a hole. A misheard lyric
that shrinks the knife. Would I can't, would

I won't. I don't know why
this violence. If I had—my bend

and bow, arrow, string. Not even worth
a kick of dirt. Nothing's so suggestive

as an empty nail. Gutted instrument.
One song lunges into you, and another's a lantern

drawling a path to your screened porch
where the drunks used to drift at night.

Howls and harmonica, lanolin light
in the windows as if it could repair something.

KEEP

Fear of summer plowed under. Fear of the
windbreak maples nothing but structure. Fear
of secrecy in the choreography of crows

gleaning kernels cast along the tracks.
A hometown evaporates into the reek inside
his homecoming helmet. The nailed-shut

door to the servants' back staircase. Defunct
coop with its scattering of hackles.
Rustle of stalks out back, long nights

lit by a firefly jar—how light and possible
a seed seems, compared to the heavy harvest.
Fear of tendrils. Of microscopic seams

bound to be swollen open. Fear of the father.
Fear of the face close enough to fail.
His thumbnail clouded blue from bad aim

with the hammer. The blot of it against her neck.
How the porch bulb, clotted with flies, inverts in her
pendant as he leans near, second-thinks the kiss, but gives it still.

In the Abandoned Church

Out there: bats shuddered the juniper,
addled the lilac's cardiac leaves.

Singe of horizon, each gone day
a letter it's relieved to burn.

Inside, no crucifix or altar,
blank lectern—just accumulate dust

felting itself back toward form.
Of course any ghosts stayed

bloused in corners, nothing but
shoulders, a lung shape, a drape

of cold blue. To see you coming,
I had to peer through

some apostle's cobalt robe,
the gibbous yellow halo

of an angel, Christ's wilted ankle
and swollen, sandaled toe. I couldn't

find plain sky, no angle not netted
with lead. Of course no voices

petted my nape, no ragged hem
cobwebbed my knees—though I was

no less ghosted by approach,
the lilt of *en route*, that absence

(slack pocket, drilled cavity)
a twitching inch from touch.

The way spirit suggests a hard need
for flesh. I wanted you tentatively

knuckling the door. In my hand,
the key's raw edge. Its blood smell.

Ex Fractura Miraculum

When the lawnmower nicks the rabbits' nest the Lord
is oiled blade is downy socket is the knot of kits writhing
like wrung hands, because who'll believe

holy without a broken body, a wound a room
you can move in and out of, though my own I never
wanted to leave, not for the yard (the smallness

of the blood, my cuffs crosshatched with clippings) or
what's beyond (wrens skim in from the margins,
banners of errata in their beaks), knowing I'm no better

than my ancestors (their mouthfuls of Pentecost),
my ministers (those outpatients of heaven), impulses
equally parochial, pickled, brined with denial, my best

murders internal (though I collapse the sod, catacomb
them, skein of bones so slight they'll quickly mince) and
who'll mistake me for an empty chamber a filed incisor

for one who sutured more than severed when they see
(the warble of petrol, my thumb at the throttle) the lawn
sealed over, flat as an altar, all injuries crypted beneath.

PALIMPSEST

No one can delete
                    inconvenience from the decalogue.

What I covet,
         what I lack: a serious kiss,

a sermon of teeth. Hands
                   at my ribcage, and the answering
incandescence in my chest.

———

The Lord's no sparrow thistling the grass. Not even
the grain of linen
               or gleaned wheat, fat

braid of kernels at the head
of a flimsy stalk. The Lord is no

medallion but a branded crest,
                  sear of coal.

———

                O
my people, our blood turned
               milk. All of our babies

born soiled, sour. The Lord is butchered
                    hides, uneven skins

pegged to studs, is rendered
and pasted into spines

               that unbind themselves, signatures

relaxing from the desiccate mucilage.

———

Lord, what have I

        but you if you'll have me? No one

can scrape or milk-soak this skin,
make your mark gone.

Rictus

My ilk can't quit lacking—
in forests, our hearts fashionably

microscopic, we pack our teeth
with willow bark, then lumber

toward each other, paws like
built-in boxing gloves, too clumsy

to touch in a way that means anything.

———

To progress, we aim for
augury. As if within the owl,

each feather's tip inscribes
a fortune, a future. Directions

we might angle in. How delicate
our steps seem, etched in the dark

air inside birds.

———

Not developing resistance to
below-the-belt rot's our first

glitch. Doesn't desire steam us
sterile as an autoclaved needle?

Primitive, we dip our instruments
in liquor, swipe them through fire,

desperate to scrub and numb.

———

The ones with fewer feelings
we trust to make the incisions.

Calm-handed. Undisturbed
by how, when they breach

our disinfected skin,
every organ, shuddering, seems

to hide a heart inside.

———

We name each feathered creature
by its signature measure.

Omit the syrinx, and
the songbird seems

hollow as its marrow,
though still the vacant throat

chapels open in hope.

———

The secret of beautiful
things being attrition,

I abandon my plan to become
the first curable amputee—

no longer certain an embrace
from strange arms would improve

on my own.

———

This wish again: permanent
reversal. Not the jaw jacked wide

in high-frequency howl. Not these
tendons twinging in reach. I never pressed

a knitbone poultice to your shoulder.
Never saw a white dress

hanging from a sword.

REMNANT

Spoiled perfume of the osage hedge
palsied with wind. Leaves unpinned.

The storm's dodge and attack—slate
congestion of clouds oncoming all

day without a punchline, the way illness
chases illness, dogging the body

with too much or too little until the fever
shivers open.

I don't know how to stay
still when the air, the same air

flexing our cells—red for breath,
white to heal—keeps taking apart

the barns, switching branches
against windows, meddling thorns

until they hitch—crossed swords.
The friction that grafts us

together. That shreds us, our flesh
flayed with loss. Our heaviest fruit

fallen, half-split by impact, releasing
the dark flock of seeds churched within.

HERE SPECIAL SUPPLICATIONS, INTERCESSIONS, AND PRAYERS MAY BE MADE

Lord, please say what happened to that chimney
abandoned in a Dakota field, and to my friend

who found it? *Wake up*, he said,
stopping the car. Careful oval stones ascended

each other's shoulders against a November sky
so steely that dark wings of geese

clanged like clappers in a heavy bell.
I remember how he lifted from the ground

the limp form of a fallen hawk, and I touched
its wings, which hung loose, delicately

unhinged. Unto thee, unto thee, unto
thee only does the soul rise

from the body. I remember him holding
me from behind. The soft words he spoke

against my hair. Teach me, Lord, to be
like the grass that surrounded us there: yielded

to wind, but weirdly alert, wild
in its reaching—

4

PRAYER

An acorn unfurls
a tail, tucked under
its argyle cap, and goes
after something smaller
than itself to stow.
Everything wild to own.
Lord, please: full-
pocket me. I want
good greed, a new
breed of wing.
I heard of a man
who affixes whiskers
to maple seeds, furring
them with tiny cattail
collars. Winter-coating
the woods. If, Lord,
you were to return, could you
be more thorn? On a stem
usually neutral—a single
spire steepling from its side.
Forests face inward. When
I pass through, the path
retracts behind me, my shadow
tender underfoot. Path that
arrows as if toward
an altar, but ends
instead in a clearing:
floral, whirring, fastened
invisibly together.

DISLOCATION

The sky drowned long ago, but we keep breathing
into its cyanotic mouth. We make the sounds we believe
heaven must make—gilt edged, buoyant. We worry

over air sacrificed during a kiss. It's hard not to
close our faces tight as gates. The tiny clasps of lockets
clicking shut, trapping images of the beloved. Remember

when a saltshaker was worth more than a chandelier?
Chasing ounces of cinnamon over oceans, everything
conceivable in pursuit of the kingdom—we called

the hairline fracture of smoke ascending from
each wrecked dwelling an oblation. Now everywhere
the temperature accelerates. We try shedding layers

but find beneath our robes more robes. On our fingers,
facets engineered to dispense light only consume it,
channeling toward a vanishing point. We begin again

assuming an expedition. First we bring back
the maps—quaintly calligraphed on skin, cities
named for long-gone wives and daughters,

saints and flowers. We salt our meat. We work
in pairs. The animals head for the sea, which is
heading for the animals.

Ash Wednesday

What became of wild
        belief? Scribes said

of Catherine, if fire were applied
to her skin,
        she felt nothing,

so strong the interior

burn. Dark blood from her mouth, and her body
        branded black.

Could we eat nothing
        save sacrament?
Could we awaken

to the smoldering
        lace edge of a pillowcase and know
                we were bound
for the pyre?

When it begins—in the salt, in the belly—child
as mote, then olive, violet, unfolding—child

as replica of an ark, thing built
        against the flood
that wants the world.

        The one who will be fragrant

in flames, immune until pierced
in the chest, and the dove
        escapes, and blood
           is enough
to quench the blaze.

Could it be
that we're chosen?

In the outskirts, the forest, a rock wall
weaves between oaks.

A man leans against the gray
chill of it. Covers his face.

According

In my mouth the name of God an overripe pear: a grain, a grit
on the tongue. A grail, all vowel-shaped gaps, like lipping the rim
of an empty cup, that low-frequency opening undoing, unhinging

the jaw. God's name as eyetooth, meat-intended, a visible
skeletal hint. God as salve for chalk. For the bent heart, the desire
that my desires would move in unison as fish. For a fox seems free,

but he's leashed to each rabbit. To the bustle in a hen's throat.
For sometimes an oak upended by unbearable wind
exposes a rib cage rooted in, for we forget

who's interred where once the crosses disappear—the unearthed
remains indistinguishable, no matter what loves or aches
once marked the softer, vanished parts. For even enduring yearning

can't scrimshaw into marrow. The mercy of a wish's eventual
hush. God's name inhabiting the pauses
between consonants, those intercostal lulls, omissions

when written but bound, once voiced, to sinew in.

Even So, Come

Grief encamps everywhere,
even in the tender

stable of your breath—
nesting the backmost

caried molar until its silver
fillings radio the same tunes

broadcast to astronauts, aliens:
songs formless as infants' dreams,

an unbreathable atmosphere.
Grief volatile as a fetal cell,

as a feeling harbored for
a girl seen once and only

once, standing outside
the middle school, oxygen

invisibly delivered
through a silicone cannula

pronging her nostrils. Hello
parable, story sequestered

in seed, only available
if your soul's already gone

out-of-body, launched
its starry ounce, immoderate

as an iris, toward a hunch
that God, as promised, is.

Enough grief leaves you
wheel-seeing, Ezekieled,

gaze brassy and feather-fanned
with images impenetrable as Patmos:

The sun sackcloth black. The moon's
broken scroll. Skies like trays

of honey, long-tombed, needing
only spit to lure them back

from artifact to sustenance. Holy
ossuary, say how this world

ends in beginning again
again. Grief as tribe,

grief as beast. Grief
counting horses on the horizon.

VIA DECUMANA

The ghosts proceeding on their knees: previously
a lower road.

———

          To ghost as habit—what am I

missing? Those assigned to nightgowns.
Those who can't release their grip on swords.

Even alive, I keep returning to scenes, rutting my way
through earth's dirty offices. Aloft, a sericulture of cirrus

     swifting the asbestos sky.

———

                  Contrails of precedence,
the ghosts lessen morningly. What am I missing?

A Rome lit by swaddled stakes dunked sulfur
so fire survives water,

        as ghosts avoid loss

via ether: zero neutering any attempted division.

———

     Ghosts as aspirate, striations remaining
after air vampires moisture from marrow.

———

Any room or road can snag a ghost; any moment

     the sky might perforate, gauzing open its grid

of here and then. I go again and again
down on the dingy linen of my knees—prayers

for the missing, ghosts for my ghosts. Necromantic
descants pacing my tongue until the harrowed clouds

relent and scrabble ash back to flesh.

Eating Oranges in the Chapel

The things of this world must be held
the careful way this girl I love balances
an orange in the brief cradle of her palms.

When her thumbs split the peel, scent
sparks the air; the sanctuary
is a window thrown open,

varnish and marble veined with ripe light,
each backlit segment of fruit a live
coal crossing her lips. The priest

seems unaware, standing in the apse—a shield
to guard Christ's suspended body,
its hasty red signatures at ankle and wrist.

When she pauses to sing
a hymn, her body sways
gently, as if given over to wind.

Her sticky hand in mine is a rescued
golden coin, and the words

unroll over us as a bandage, as though
we're anything but abandoned.

RECOVERY

Foreground sorrow and the world
      reels and blues. Your side effects,

your inability to alter
      the weather. Your alphabet

as names of hurricanes. The scritch of
      lace against lace. In your illness, unable

to imagine your skin not
      scored by knives, scoured by fever,

you said thanks to the sea
      for keeping its bones at the bottom.

You said tell me again the one.
      When I sang for someone's wife the night

before she died, I could tell
      she knew it was her last moon—

full, too, a lacteal pool. A nurse
      waited knitting in the kitchen.

I've never known a nearer Lord.
      You said are you more afraid

of losing things, or giving them away?
      I said the one about the pickled egg.

The jukebox. Iodine. The last time
      I felt weightless. Blueberry pie. Zanzibar.

Let Them Be Left

What we deem weeds
flower in dank
shades—mustard, owl
brown, furred
saffron with pollen,
fierce to attach
to the sinus.

I float
hip deep in
corrugated stems;
I serve

as distribution system
for the passive
barbs of nettles,
a secondhand
sting. I know God

understands the upside-
down scars
of the shepherd:
God launching a burr
as lure into the world,
God frightened for
the whole quiet season.

These weeds, lovely
women in plain coats
beneath a surefire prophecy
of air: you will walk

on the wind and be
sown. Cast over
rough waters, stuck
to frayed cuffs, you will
fear not, for nothing
latched can be lost.

I wish I'd carried more,
and farther. I wish all
those dun blooms
would fox their plumed
errors into my arms.

Yes I Said Yes

Promise me every blossom
as the vulva's dusky proxy,

center-stabbed with ferrous
thread, as in knit together,

as in stitches to be licked until
dissolving. Promise an edible

dark, lapses in landscape—
selvage verge of the field

interrupted. Tart drape
of osage. Promise a bower.

Promise no curse. No gate
at the garden. Loose horses.

Milk lyric of the moon, O,
all the perfume, all the perfume

from all of the jars.

OFFERING

Quiet provision of horses, sky
chamois-soft, tired as prayer.
Privacy of the tongue

until it keys against
teeth to speak.
All morning needing

to be fed or freed—
Christ who doubles
the insides of barrels,

who traces a curse
in the dirt to extract
the splinter at its heart.

I know inhabiting
a ballad binds us
to the sheet-music sorrow

of a Sunday parlor,
a magnolia's glossy,
Sabbath-white legato.

So many songs that hide
a murder inside. A love
forever horizoned. Christ

saying, When you heal, wait
before you say it was me.
Christ pasturing his hands.

NOTES

"Prayer [The evangelical exotic-dance instructor considers it]" is dedicated to Kari Spreeman.

"God Exists" is after Yusef Komunyakaa's "Corrigenda."

"Your Heart Your Wobble" borrows from the Dick Justice song "Henry Lee."

"Keep" owes its "Fear of . . ." anaphora to Lytton Smith's "The Tightrope Walker's Childhood."

"Prayer [An acorn unfurls]" alludes to the botanical manipulations of artist Jim Proctor.

"Via Decumana" is inspired by Wes Burdine's writing about the York Roman Soldiers.

"Let Them Be Left" draws its title from Gerard Manley Hopkins's "Inversnaid."

ACKNOWLEDGMENTS

The following poems first appeared, some in earlier versions, in these publications:

Elixir: "Ash Wednesday"
Gettysburg Review: "Icarian," "Palimpsest," and "See Coast Hurrying
 into Sea"
Hotel Amerika: "God Exists" and "Poustinia"
Image: "According," "Altricial," and "Salt Wife"
Kenyon Review: "Let Them Be Left" and "Prayer [An acorn unfurls]"
The Other Journal: "Marrow"
Poetry City U.S.A., VOLUME 3: "Keep"
Revolver: "The One Sentence You Send Me from Wisconsin Concerns
 Chickens"
Rock & Sling: "Eating Oranges in the Chapel," "Face of Clay,"
 "Here Special Supplications, Intercessions, and Prayers May Be
 Made," and "Remnant"
Theopoetics: "Amor"
Third Coast: "Acts of God"
Water~Stone: "Corsetry"
West Branch: "Congenital" and "Where Were You First Introduced to the
 Spirit?"

"Congenital" was featured on Verse Daily (posted online March 12, 2014).

"Icarian" was featured on Poetry Daily (posted online August 20, 2013).

"Acts of God" appears in *Poems + Prints,* published in 2010 by Laura Brown in conjunction with the Minnesota Center for Book Arts.

I am grateful to each editor who has selected my work and sent it out into the world, as well as to the readers who have received it.

I am also grateful to the organizations that have generously supported my work through fellowships, grants, and residencies: the Anderson Center, Banfill-Locke Center for the Arts, the Jerome Foundation, the McKnight Foundation, the University of Northwestern—St. Paul, and the Virginia Center for the Creative Arts.

My deep gratitude, too, to all who have helped me, directly and indirectly, in the making of this book:

To Paisley Rekdal, for choosing my manuscript, and to everyone at Tupelo—especially Jim Schley and Bronwyn Becker—for shepherding it into shape.

To my teachers, who've been models, mentors, guides—especially Walter Pennington, for complimenting my words way back when; Meg Papadolias, for years of immersion in beautiful songs; David L. Johnson, for listening patiently; Jonathan Johnson, for his buoyant spirit and intense attention to drafts and to humans; Nance Van Winckel, for her expansive creativity and keen pen; Christopher Howell, for his humor and deep, wise kindness; and Judith Hougen, for pretty much everything—early and ongoing influence, abiding friendship, cat adoption, you name it.

To my MFA community at the Inland Northwest Center for Writers, for two cherished years of inspiration, formation, and fun—and to Linda Cooper, Ginger Grey, Kat Smith, Laura Stott Rogers, and Emily Van Kley, for continuing to be rigorous readers and long-distance accomplices.

To my colleagues at the University of Northwestern—St. Paul, for their support.

To my students, for surprising me every time with their particular voices, vision, and insight.

To my family at Mercy Seat, for the thoughtful synthesis of art, theology, and worship, and for hands-on help in times of change and need.

To Dave Harrity, for his astute eye, relentless advocacy, and for being kindred.

To my family, for their love, and for being my blood.

To my William, for showing up near the end of this story, bringing—and being—a joy that can't be housed by words.

And, finally, to Scott—for laying hands on every page of this book, for reminding me to look up, and for loving me as I've been, as I am, and as I will be.

OTHER BOOKS FROM TUPELO PRESS

See our complete list at www.tupelopress.org

WASECA-LE SUEUR
REGIONAL LIBRARY
SYSTEM
408 North State Street
Waseca, MN 56093

CPSIA information can be obtained
at www.ICGtesting.com
Printed in the USA
LVOW06s0756030217
523131LV00029B/847/P